MY FIRST REFERENCE LIBRARY

THE BODY

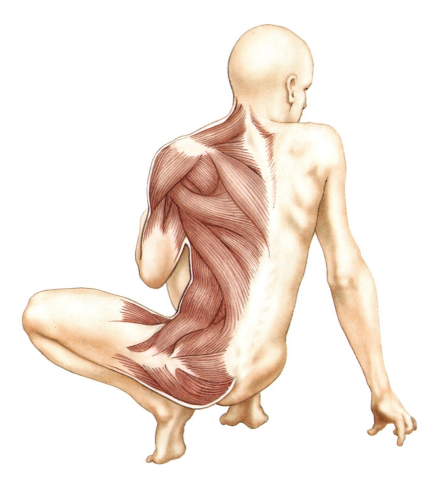

by Julie Brown and Robert Brown
Adapted from Brian J. Ford's
The Human Body

BELITHA PRESS

First published in Great Britain in 1990 by
Belitha Press Limited
31 Newington Green, London N16 9PU
Copyright © Belitha Press Limited and
Gareth Stevens, Inc. 1990
Illustrations/photographs copyright © in this
format by Belitha Press Limited and Gareth
Stevens, Inc. 1990
All right reserved. No part of this book may be
reproduced or utilized in any form or by any
means, electronic or mechanical, including
photocopying, recording or by any information
storage and retrieval system, without permission
in writing from the Publisher.
ISBN 1 85561 040 X
Typeset by Chambers Wallace, London
Printed in the UK for Imago Publishing
by MacLehose and Partners

British Library Cataloguing in Publication Data
CIP data for this book is available from the British
Library

Acknowledgements

Photographic credits:

Biophoto Associates 10, 12, 15, 32, 37, 41 bottom, 44
Colorsport 53 top, 47 bottom, 49
Sally and Richard Greenhill 13, 23, 50 left
Steven Fuller 47 top
The Hutchison Library 5, 59
Camilla Jessel 43, 51
Oxford Scientific Films 52
Queen Victoria Hospital, East Grinstead 53 bottom
Science Photo Library, 7, 17, 29, 31, 39, 41 top, 50 right, 56
Spectrum Colour Library 9, 35 bottom
The Tate Gallery, London 21
University College Hospital, London, School of Dentistry 55
John Watney 19

Illustrated by: Frank Kennard and Eugene Fleury

Series editors: Neil Champion and Mark Sachner
Educational consultant: Carolyn Kain
Editors: Kate Scarborough and Rita Reitci
Designed by: Groom and Pickerill
Picture research and art editing: Ann Usborne
Specialist consultant: Dr Margaret Rostron

Contents

Chapter One
The Human Shape
The Body	4
Bones	6
The Skull	8

Chapter Two
Centres of Life
The Brain	10
The Nerves	12
The Liver	14
Blood	16
The Lungs	18

Chapter Three
The Senses
Eyes	20
Ears	22
Taste and Smell	24
The Skin and Touch	26

Chapter Four
The Food System
The Mouth	28
The Throat	30
The Stomach	32
The Gut	34
Waste Matter	36

Chapter Five
Glands
The Thymus	38
The Third Eye	40
The Thyroid	42
The Pancreas	44

Chapter Six
Movement
Muscles	46
Reflexes	48
The Heart	50

Chapter Seven
On The Outside
Hair	52
Nails	54
Teeth	56

Chapter Eight
Babies
Giving Birth	58
Glossary	60
Index	62

Words found in **bold** are explained in the glossary on pages 60 and 61

CHAPTER ONE
THE HUMAN SHAPE

The Body

Your body is made of flesh and bone, blood and water. It is not 'a machine'. It knows how to feed itself and how to keep the right amount of water inside. Sometimes your body moves faster than you can think. And you do not have to think to make your heart beat. Your body can do many things that a computer cannot do. For example, your body has begun to read this book.

▼ Humans start growing before they are born. Babies grow the fastest. By the age of 18, most humans have nearly stopped growing.

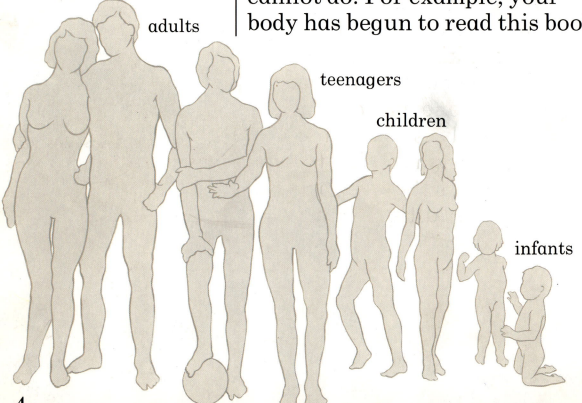

adults

teenagers

children

infants

Cells

Humans begin life as a **cell** in their mother's body. This first cell is about the size of a full stop. Soon, the cell divides into two cells. The cells continue to divide and different kinds of cells begin to be made. Some cells become skin, others bone, muscles, or hair. Your body is a huge mass of cells: each is a tiny living thing. If each cell does its job properly, you will be a healthy human being.

▲ The Latin name for human beings is Homo sapiens. This means wise man. There are many races of humans.

▼ The first cell is called an egg. It grows inside the mother. The egg divides and different kinds of cells are made. Here are examples of a few.

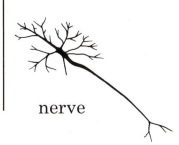

nerve

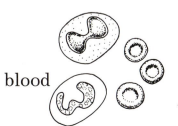

blood

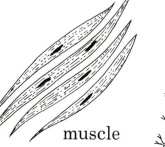

muscle

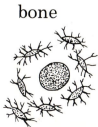

bone

THE HUMAN SHAPE

Bones

▶ Your skeleton gives your body strength. Muscles are fastened onto it, so you can move. Your bones also store calcium. If you don't eat enough calcium, your bones will become weak.

Facts and Feats

● Each arm has 32 bones. There are 31 in each leg. 14 bones make up your face.

● Boys usually stop growing at the age of 18 and girls at 16½. Up to the age of 30 you will gain another 4 mm. After 50, you will slowly begin to shrink.

● Bone is mostly made of a stony material.

● The human skeleton contains the same number of bones as a horse.

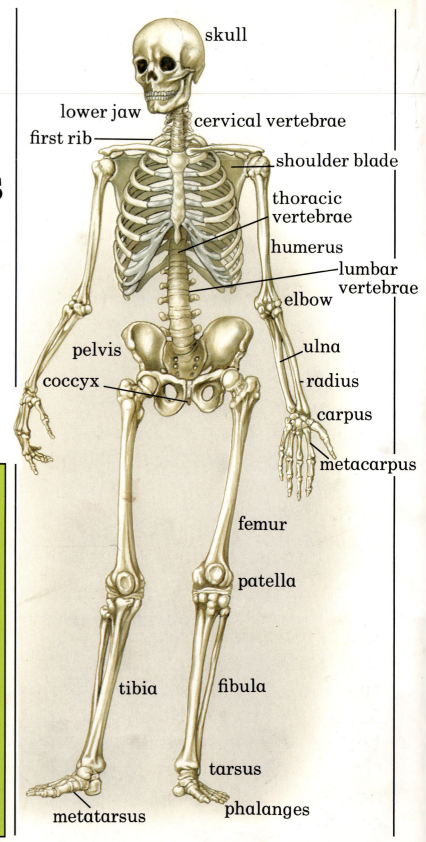

There are over 300 bones in a baby's body. As the baby grows, some bones join together. Adults have only about 220 bones.

Types of bone
Long bones: these are the bones in your arms and legs.
Short bones: the bones in your fingers and toes.
Flat bones: some parts of your body are protected by flat bones, such as the skull and pelvis (hip bone).
Irregular bones: inside your hands, feet and ears there are many oddly-shaped bones.

The spine
Your spine is divided into 33 tubular bones called vertebrae. Each one has a hole down its side. The **spinal cord** runs down a separate arch at the back of your vertebrae and is protected by them. Your vertebrae have parts that stick out called processes. Muscles join onto these. At the bottom of your spine are a few tiny vertebrae. In some other animals these are the start of a tail.

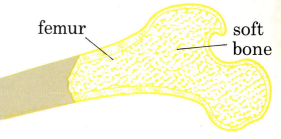
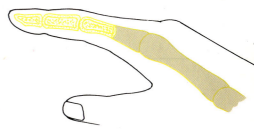

▲ The outside of the thigh bone is strong. Inside it is more spongy. The finger bone is also hard on the outside and spongy inside. Red blood cells are made inside these bones.

▼ This x-ray shows the bones in the hand and wrist.

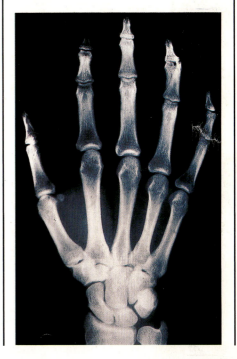

THE HUMAN SHAPE

The Skull

▶ This is the skull of a healthy person. It has strong bones and no signs of tooth decay.

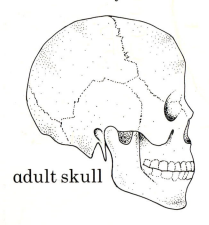

adult skull

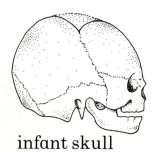

infant skull

▲ There is not much difference between an infant and an adult skull. But in the infant's skull the bones still have to join together.

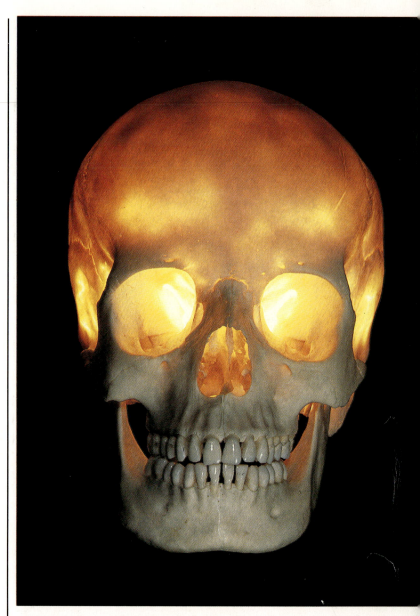

The skull begins as many rounded, flat bones. These bones join together after you are born. The lower jaw is the only part of the skull that can move. Two round sockets hold the eyes. The delicate parts inside your ear are protected by the rounded sides of your skull.

Parts of the skull

Four thick, tough bones form the front and back of the skull. When you are born these bones are not joined together. You can feel a soft spot on the head of a baby where the space between the bones is. In adults the bones are locked together tightly. The edges of the separate bones join at a wavy line, known as a suture. This makes the skull very strong. Two more bones around the side of the skull help to protect the brain. Beneath are the cheekbones and jaw bones.

▼ Pirate ships flew a flag showing a skull and crossbones. It was meant to scare people. Today this symbol is used as a warning sign on bottles of poison.

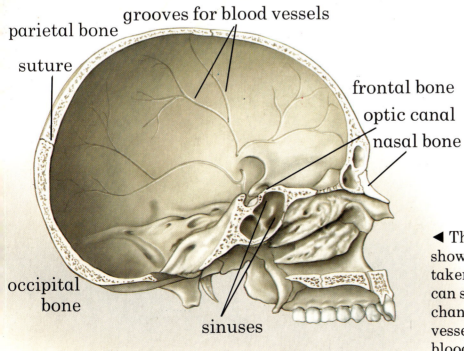

◀ This section of a skull shows the large space taken up by the brain. You can see some of the channels where blood vessels pass. These carry blood to the skull.

CHAPTER TWO
CENTRES OF LIFE

The Brain

Brain diagram labels: cerebral cortex, parietal lobe, frontal lobe, occipital lobe, cerebrum, corpus callosum, pineal gland, optic chiasma, pituitary gland, temporal lobe, medulla oblongata, cerebellum

▶ The human brain is soft. The 'thinking' part is the outer layer.

▼ These brain cells have been stained purple to make them show up better.

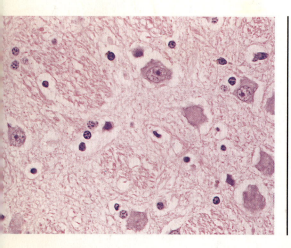

There are about 15 thousand million cells in the human brain. The size of the brain has little to do with intelligence. The human brain is not the biggest in the world. For example, an elephant's brain is larger than a human's.

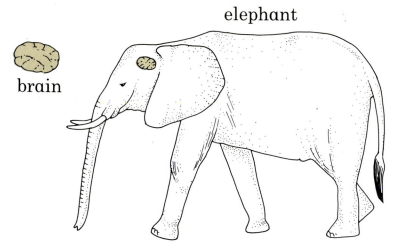
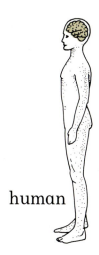

Brain cells

Brain cells die off every day and are never replaced. Every time you learn something it is stored in the brain as a pattern of cells. As you learn more so more links are formed between the brain cells. The pattern grows more complex. Even if some brain cells die, still the overall pattern remains.

Areas of the brain

In the front of your brain are the frontal **lobes**. They contain areas that make you move and behave as you do. At the back of the brain is the cerebellum. This controls your co-ordination. Intelligence lies in the outer layer of the brain. This outer layer is so big in humans that it has to be wrinkled up to fit inside the skull. This layer is called the cerebral cortex.

▲ Some large animals have larger brains than humans. For example, elephants have much bigger brains than humans. But they are not as intelligent. Their outer 'thinking' layer is not so large.

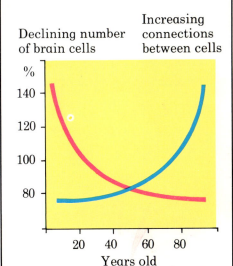

▲ Brain cells die off as you get older. But at the same time more connections will have formed. This means an older person has more information stored away.

CENTRES OF LIFE

The Nerves

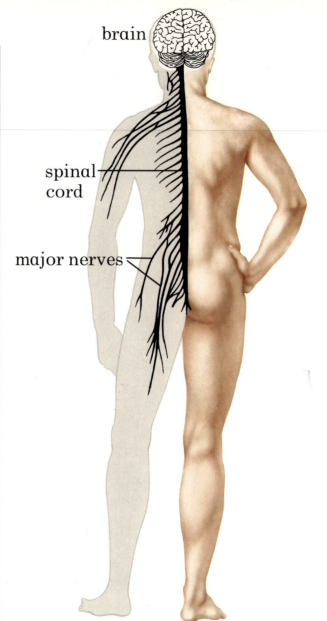

brain

spinal cord

major nerves

▶ The brain is connected to the rest of the body by the spinal cord. This main nerve is protected by bones in the spine called vertebrae. A pair of nerves comes out of the spine between each vertebra.

▼ A brown stain has been used to show these nerve cells. The long arms reach out to other nerve cells.

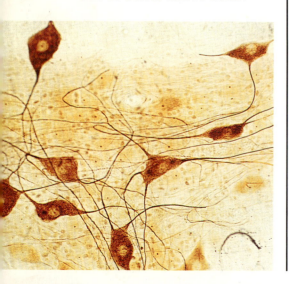

Nerves are long white cells that stretch through the body. They take signals from one part of the body to another. Nerve cells are very close together, but do not actually touch. The small gaps between them are called synapses. Chemicals pass the signals from one nerve to another.

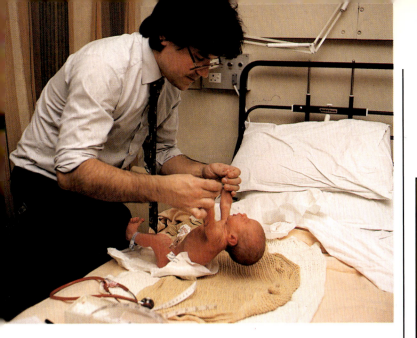

◀ Many actions (like holding onto a doctor's fingers) are reflexes.

Did you know?

● Nerve cord branches (axons) grow at a rate of 4 mm a day.

● A person's brain contains billions of nerve cells. An ant's brain has only about 250.

● 44 pairs of nerves run down from the spinal cord to the rest of the body.

Reflexes

Many signals from your nerves go straight to your brain. If you have an itch, for instance, it's up to you whether or not you scratch it. Reflexes are different. Here the signals pass straight from one set of nerves to another without going through the brain. If pepper gets up your nose, you sneeze. It's not like an itch because you cannot stop yourself from doing it. This is an example of a reflex action.

Spinal cord

Most nerves join together to form the spinal cord that runs through your backbone. If this cord is **severed**, your body will not work properly below the damaged area.

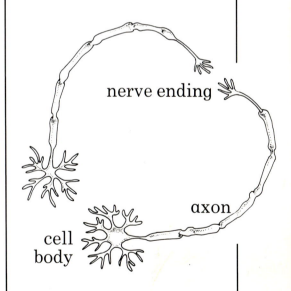

▲ Nerve cells send out many branches to gather information. But only one long branch, called an axon, sends signals.

13

CENTRES OF LIFE

The Liver

The liver is the largest **gland** in the body. It weighs about 1½ kg and is brown or purplish red in colour. The liver is protected by the lower part of your ribs. It stretches right across the body. It is up to 15 centimetres thick.

The living organ

The liver has a good name because it makes you live. The food you eat is changed into useful energy in the liver. Blood coming from the liver is always warm. This helps heat your body. Poisonous things in the blood are broken down in the liver. Your

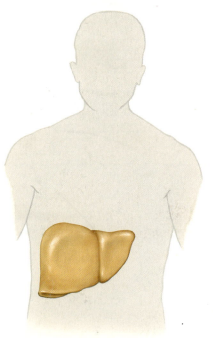

▲ The liver lies across your body just inside the lower part of your ribs.

▶ In your liver, there is a greenish bag called the gall bladder. It produces bile which helps you break down fatty and oily food into useful energy.

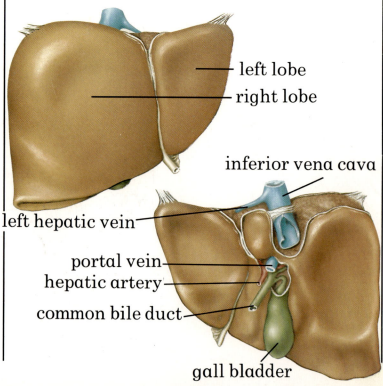

- left lobe
- right lobe
- inferior vena cava
- left hepatic vein
- portal vein
- hepatic artery
- common bile duct
- gall bladder

liver also makes vitamin A from carotene, which is found in vegetables such as carrots. A **virus** infection in the liver can be very serious because the liver is so important to life. The liver can also be damaged by too much alcohol.

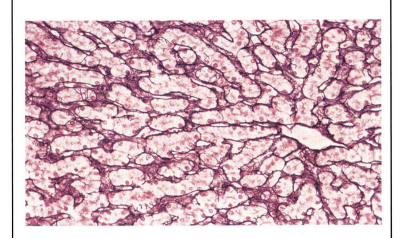

A purple stain has been used so you can see how liver cells form spaces. Blood flows through these spaces. On its way, it picks up useful substances and gets rid of waste. The liver then deals with these. The blood moves through spaces in the liver. It doesn't stay in the blood vessels. In this way the blood cells can contact the liver cells correctly. ◀

▼ This diagram gives a clearer idea of the movement of blood in the liver.

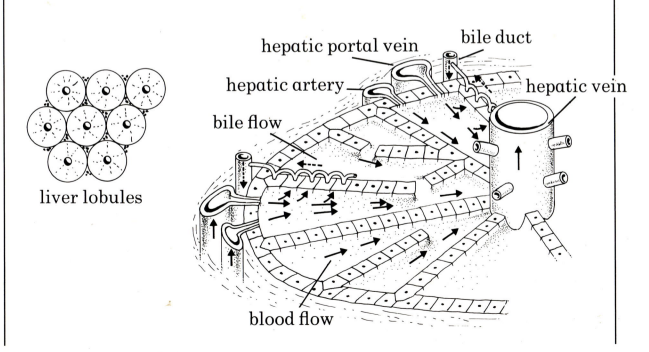

CENTRES OF LIFE

Blood

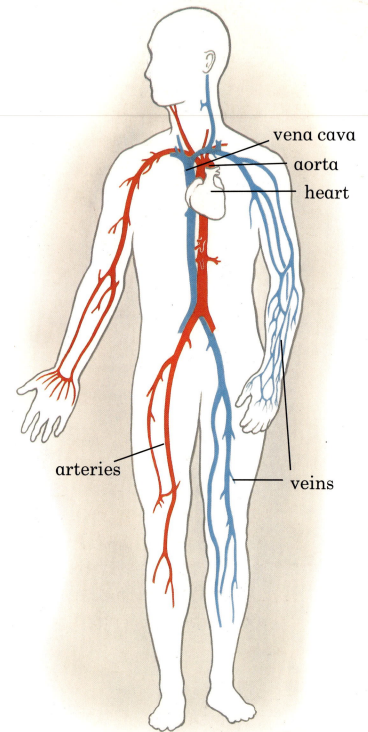

▶ Blood moves out into the body through arteries (red). The blood returns to the heart through veins (blue). There are, of course, veins and arteries on both sides of the body.

Did you know?

● The artery that runs from your heart, the aorta, is as thick as a garden hose.

● People used to think some illnesses were caused by too much blood. Leeches were used to suck out the 'extra' blood.

● Each blood cell lives long enough to pass around your body 100,000 times.

Blood is a liquid **tissue**. There are about six litres of blood in an adult human body. There are two types of blood cells: red and white.

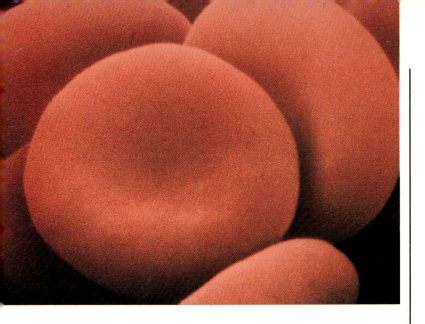

◀ Red blood cells are about 2½ thousandths of a millimetre thick. White blood cells are transparent and can be many different shapes. Tiny particles in the blood that stop you bleeding are called platelets. They clot blood and help form scabs. ▼

Red blood cells

There are about 35 million million red blood cells in an adult body. Haemoglobin, a red material, gives red blood cells their colour. Haemoglobin picks up **oxygen** as it passes through the lungs and carries it through the body. Each red blood cell only lives for about four months. But new red blood cells are made in the marrow of bones and replace the dead ones.

White blood cells

For every white blood cell, there are about 600 red ones. Among other things, white cells help control infections and can destroy germs. There are several different types of white blood cell.

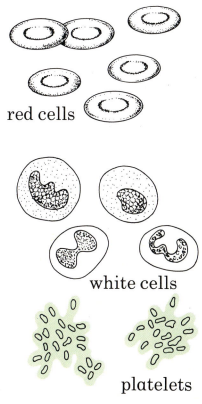

red cells

white cells

platelets

CENTRES OF LIFE

The Lungs

thyroid cartilage

main bronchi

trachea

upper lobe

upper lobe

middle lobe

lower lobe

cardiac depression

lower lobe

▶ This drawing shows what the lungs look like. The one on the right is whole. The one on the left has been cut through to show what it is like on the inside. The lungs fit tightly under the ribs with hardly any space left over. In the right lung you can see a large dent, the cardiac depression. This is where the heart fits.

The lungs are like soft, moist sponges. They are extremely delicate. In the lungs, air comes together with blood. Oxygen from the air is picked up by haemoglobin in the red blood cells and carried around the body. The windpipe leads down to the lungs. There, it divides into smaller and smaller airways that lead to thin bubbles called alveoli. Each alveolus is lined with fine blood vessels where oxygen is taken up. These blood vessels are so thin that blood cells have to squeeze through in single file.

Breathing

Adult lungs can hold 5 or 6 litres of air. But when you breathe, you normally let in (and let out) about one-tenth of this. There is always about 2 litres of air in the lungs. This keeps them inflated. As well as taking oxygen in, your lungs let out the **carbon dioxide** waste.

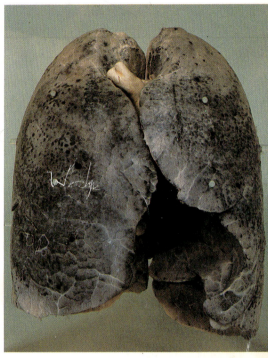

▼ These are actual human lungs. Lungs are not usually this dark colour, but these are diseased lungs. They came from a heavy smoker.

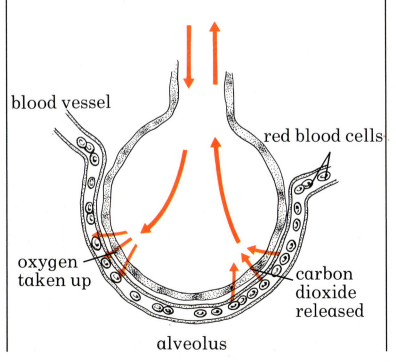

◀ The airways in the lungs get smaller and smaller until they form tiny round spongy bubbles called alveoli. This diagram shows a single alveolus. Around it move the red blood cells in their tiny blood vessels, called capillaries, collecting oxygen and giving up waste carbon dioxide.

CHAPTER THREE
THE SENSES

Eyes

Inside the eye
The human eye is very sensitive. An eye has a lens to make what we see clear. But it does not work like a camera. A camera lens slides in and out to focus. An eye lens can become thinner or thicker to bring what you see into focus.

Behind the lens, the eyeball is filled with a clear jelly called the vitreous humour. Light rays

▼ Optic nerves connect the eyes to the brain. These send signals to the brain that tell you what you are seeing. Specially arranged muscles allow the eyes to turn in many directions.

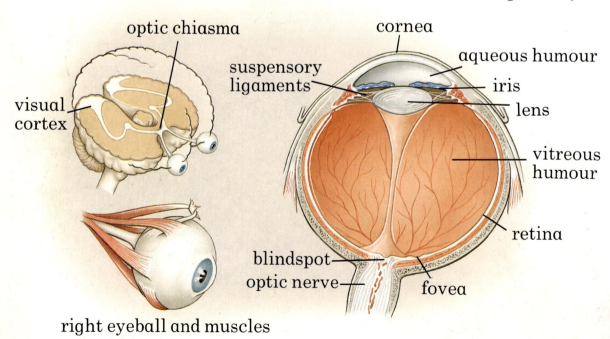

shine in through this jelly and make a pattern on the back of the eye. This part is called the retina. The retina has **cones**, which see colour in bright light, and **rods**, which see black and white in dim light. Where the eye's nerve leaves the eye to send signals to the brain, there are no rods or cones. This is called the blind spot.

Seeing and the brain

The pattern that falls on the retina is actually upside down. The brain's job is to turn the pattern around so everything looks the right way up. The eyes and brain work together to help us see properly.

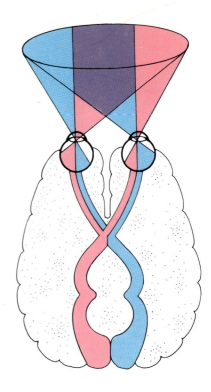

▲ This diagram shows that the brain creates one picture from the views of each eye.

Facts and Feats

● Male eyes are bigger than female eyes (by about 0.5mm).

● The pupil can open as wide as 8 mm or shrink to 1.5 mm in diameter.

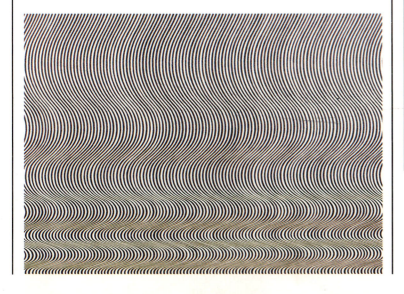

◀ If you stare at this long enough it appears to be moving. This is because your eye finds it difficult to sort out all the details.

THE SENSES

Ears

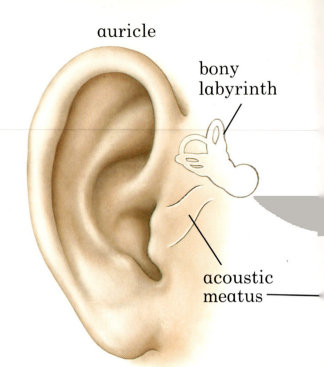

Facts and Feats

● Many mammals, such as bats and dogs, can hear much higher sounds than humans can.

● Even with your eyes shut, you can tell very accurately where sounds are coming from.

● The human ear can hear 1500 different notes, from high to low. It can also hear 350 different levels of loudness, from whispers to screams.

You probably think of your ear as one of the shell-shaped things that stick out from your head. But that is only the outside part of the ear. It collects the sounds and sends them down into the earhole. Inside the earhole are the eardrum and several tiny bones.

How we hear

Sounds hit the eardrum and make it **vibrate**. This makes the tiny bones in the ear, called ossicles, vibrate. Next the sound travels through the cochlea, which is shaped like a snail's shell. Finally the sound reaches

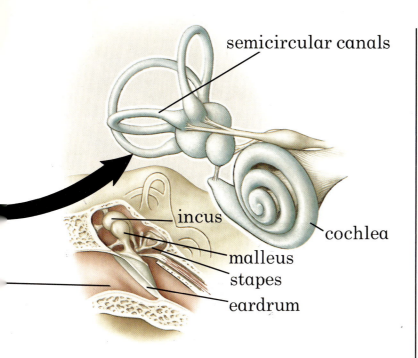

◀ The outer ear is shaped to collect sounds. Sound then travels down the ear to the eardrum. The arrow points to this area enlarged. The three ossicles are the smallest bones in the body.

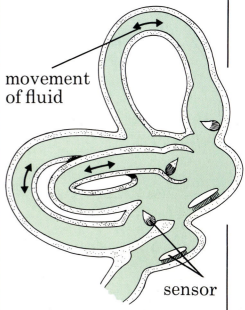

the **organ of Corti**. High sounds make the lower and larger part of the organ of Corti vibrate, and low sounds stimulate the smaller (upper) parts. Tiny nerve fibres then tell your brain what you are hearing. Very loud noises, such as pneumatic drills or loud music, can damage the organ of Corti.

▲ Every time you move your head, liquid travels around three curved canals in the inner ear. Tiny hairs in the fluid measure your movements. They help you keep your balance. If you spin around and stop suddenly, the fluid keeps on moving. This is what makes you dizzy.

◀ This Chinese acrobat's inner ear makes sure every movement keeps her on the tightrope.

THE SENSES

Taste and Smell

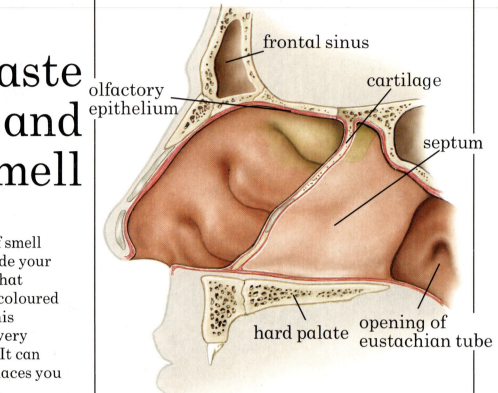

▶ Your sense of smell begins deep inside your nose. The area that detects smell is coloured pale brown in this diagram. It is a very powerful sense. It can remind you of places you visited long ago.

Different Smells
- Ethereal (fruits, beeswax)
- Resinous (lavender, cloves)
- Fragrant (flowers, perfume)
- Ambrosial (musk)
- Garlic (garlic, onion)
- Burning (tobacco, burnt hair)
- Goat (dirty socks, sweat)
- Repulsive (bedbugs)

Your sense of smell is closely related to your sense of taste. Very often what you think you are tasting you are really just smelling. If you ate an onion with your nose pinched shut, you might not know what you were eating.

Smell
Your sense of smell can detect even the smallest odour from

far away. Anything with a smell sends tiny particles into the air. If the smell is strong enough your nose picks it up. The nose then sends a signal to the brain – and the brain tells you what the smell is.

Taste

You taste things when foods or drinks touch different taste-buds in your mouth. The taste-buds also send different messages to your brain. Your brain works out what the taste is.

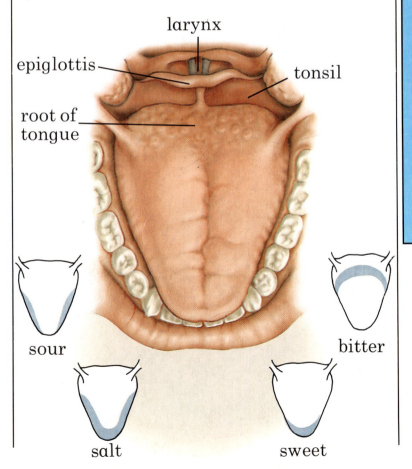

How you taste

Your tongue is covered with taste buds. There are about 9,000 of them and each one can taste only one of the four flavours. These are sweet, sour, bitter and salt. Sweet and salt are tasted by the taste-buds at the front of the tongue, bitter at the back of the tongue and sour at the sides.

The smelliest smell

One of the most revolting smells comes from a chemical made up of carbon, hydrogen and sulphur. Its smell is similar to a mixture of the smells from rotting cabbage, garlic, onions, burnt toast and sewer gas. Your sense of smell is twenty thousand times stronger than your sense of taste.

◀ Your tongue is covered with little sensors called taste-buds. Each area of the tongue can taste a different sort of flavour.

25

THE SENSES

The Skin and Touch

Facts and Feats

- The Chinese discovered that fingerprints can be used for identification 1300 years ago.

- Your fingerprint may contain an arch, a loop, a whorl, or a mixture of these.

The skin is the largest **organ** of the human body. Many nerves in the skin help us to know that things we touch are hot or cold, rough or smooth, soft or hard. Skin is an amazing organ because it does many important jobs all at once.

Temperature control

One job the skin does is to control the body's temperature. When you walk or run, your muscles give off heat. When your blood becomes too warm, the blood vessels in your skin become bigger. This lets off heat and helps to keep you cool. Your skin also helps cool you down by

▶ Your bedroom may contain thousands of these tiny creatures. They are dust mites that eat the dead skin cells that flake off your body.

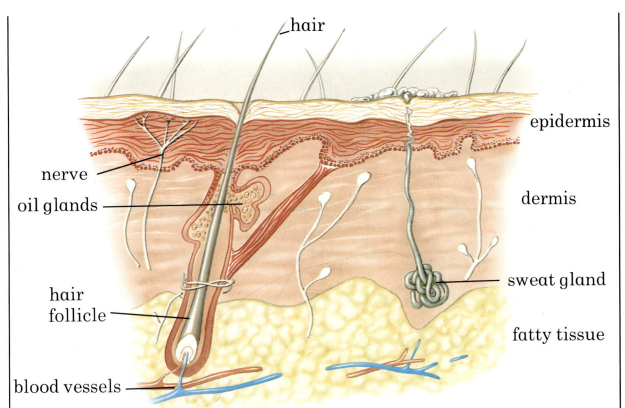

▲ Here is a cross-section diagram of human skin. The dead skin cells are on the surface. Below them are the living layers that make new cells. The skin contains nerves, hair follicles, sweat glands and oil glands.

releasing sweat from sweat glands. When this water evaporates, you feel cooler still.

Under the skin

Skin has many layers. The outer layer has dry scaly cells. These cells are dead, and they are always being shed from the surface of your skin. Under that are layers of living skin cells. There are also thousands of sensitive nerves. This layer contains the pigments that colour the skin. Underneath this is a layer of fatty tissue. It helps you to keep warm.

CHAPTER FOUR
THE FOOD SYSTEM

The Mouth

Look at your mouth in a mirror. You will notice your teeth and tongue right away. Underneath your tongue is a **membrane** called the frenulum, and veins that draw blood from the tongue. If you look at the base of the frenulum you will see a tiny opening. This is the outlet of a gland that produces **saliva**. Saliva moistens food and starts the process of **digestion**.

The Mouth

- About six weeks after the egg cell has divided the unborn baby has formed a tiny mouth.

- The lining of your mouth is made of soft cells. These are shaped like paving stones.

- Your mouth is full of tiny living things called microbes. These help to protect you from bad germs.

- Your saliva glands make 1 litre of spit per day. A cow's saliva gland produces 60 litres per day!

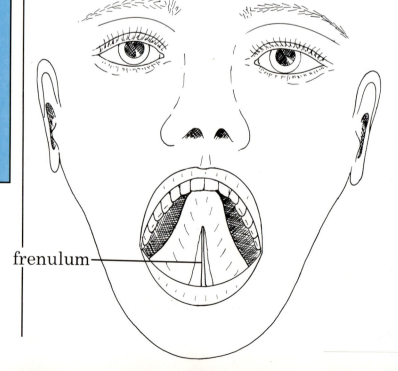

▶ The frenulum connects your tongue to the bottom of your mouth. It stops you from swallowing your tongue.

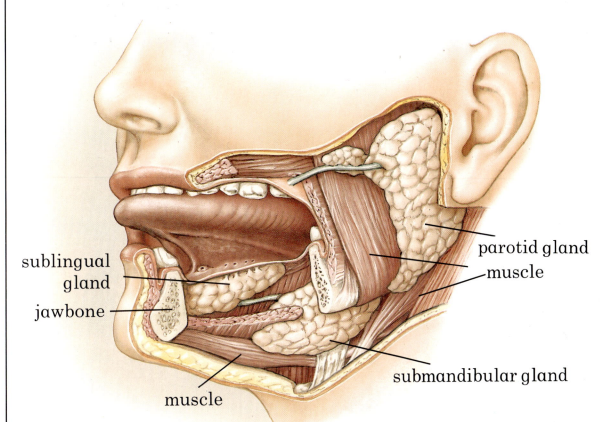

If you open your mouth wide, you will also notice the uvula. This looks like a ball hanging down at the back of your mouth. Nobody really knows what the uvula is for. On each side of your throat are the tonsils. Healthy tonsils can collect bad germs that could make you sick. Sometimes tonsils get infected and have to be removed. Also in your throat are two small openings called Eustachian tubes. These lead to the inside of the ear behind the eardrum.

▲ The tongue has many muscle bands so that you can talk and eat. Larger muscles work to help your jaws move.

THE FOOD SYSTEM

The Throat

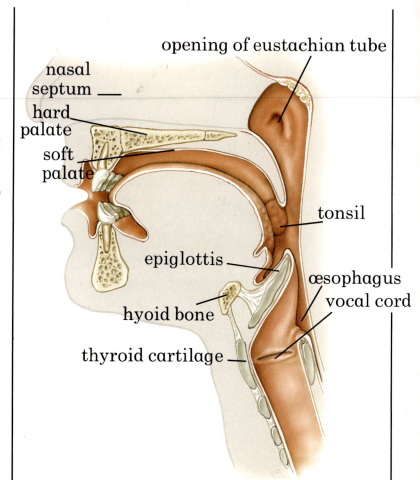

▶ You do not want air in your stomach or food in your lungs. The epiglottis stops this happening. Reflex muscles control the epiglottis so you don't have to think about using it.

Have you ever noticed that you can't swallow and breathe at the the same time? Or swallow and talk at the same moment? That is because your throat carefully controls your swallowing, breathing and talking.

Inside the throat

The upper part of your throat is called the pharynx. The upper part of your windpipe is the larynx. The throat has a very sensitive **valve** that prevents us from choking on food or swallowing air. This valve is a small trapdoor called the epiglottis. When you swallow food, the epiglottis closes off the upper part of the throat and the windpipe. Otherwise, you'd get food in your lungs!

If you touch the outside of your neck, you will feel some rings under the skin. These are bands of **cartilage** that protect your throat. Your throat also contains vocal cords. These are flaps of tissue that can be stretched like rubber bands to make different sounds.

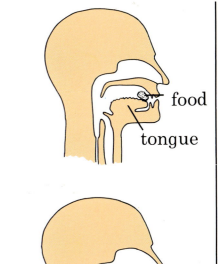
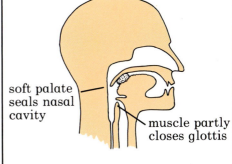
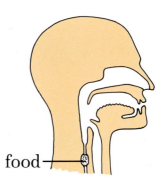

▲ Swallowing food is a very complicated act that involves many muscles.

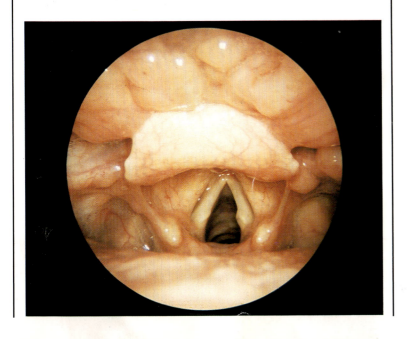

◀ In your throat are vocal cords like these. The hole you see here tightens when you speak. The epiglottis is the large white flap above the vocal cords.

THE FOOD SYSTEM

The Stomach

The stomach stretches from behind the left ribs to the belly-button. It is a flexible bag that holds food after it has been chewed and swallowed. It can hold over a litre.

The stomach in action
Throughout the day, your stomach is in motion just as if it was being gently squeezed. Food passes through the stomach within three hours of eating. The stomach also makes **hydrochloric acid**, which helps

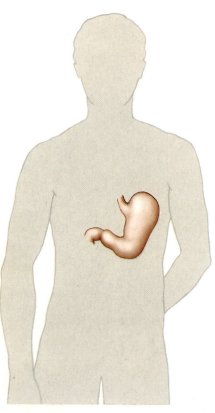

▲ This is the stomach's real position in the body. What we usually call the stomach is really the abdomen.

▶ The stomach is a flexible bag that squeezes food out to the intestines. A ring of muscle at each end helps the stomach hold food.

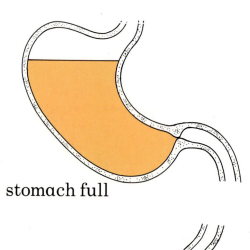

stomach full

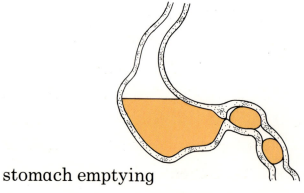

stomach emptying

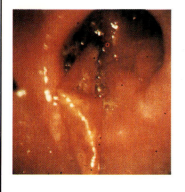
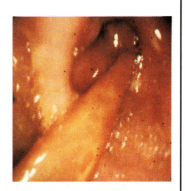
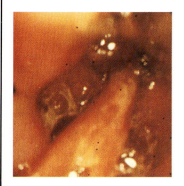
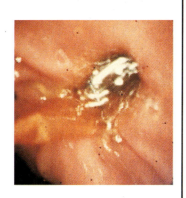

◀ These photographs show different views of the inside of a living human stomach.

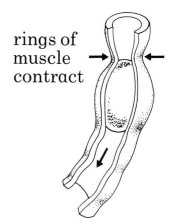

rings of muscle contract

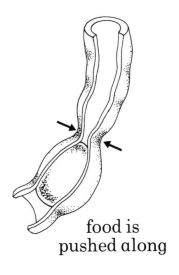

food is pushed along

▲ If you put your ear on someone's abdomen, you will hear gurgling noises as intestine muscles gently squeeze through food.

What Does the Stomach Do?
- It holds food before passing it to the intestines.
- It makes hydrochloric acid to soften the food and kill germs.
- Its muscles squeeze to help mix up the food and acid.
- It adds slippery **mucin** to help the food move through the gut.

soften food for digestion. This acid is actually strong enough to burn clothing. But the stomach wall is usually not affected. Sometimes your stomach makes too much acid. This makes a dent in the stomach's wall which is called an ulcer.

THE FOOD SYSTEM

The Gut

Once the food has left your stomach it passes to your gut or intestines. In an adult there are about 8 or 9 metres of intestines. Near the stomach is the small intestine. Next comes the large intestine.

Food for life

The intestines are always moving. They mix and push the food along. The small intestine takes the goodness out of the food mush and sends it to the liver. This goodness is made of **proteins**, **vitamins**, fats and **carbohydrates** for energy. The small intestine is lined with tiny hairs called villi. These collect

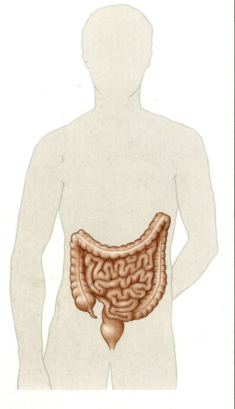

▲ Eight or nine metres of intestines are held in your abdomen! This is where food that is useful is passed on to other parts of the body.

▶ Here is a close-up view of the villi. They cover the small intestine like a velvety carpet.

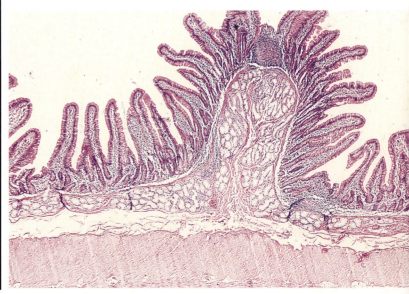

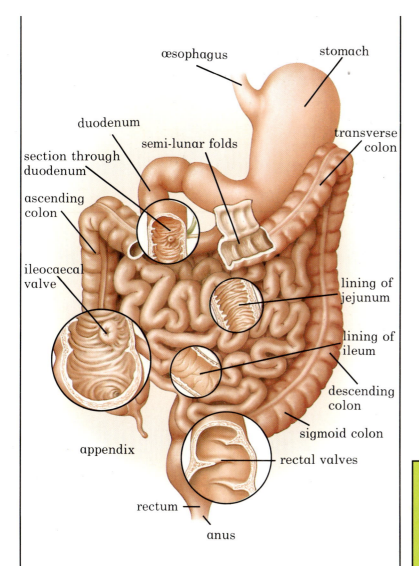

◀ After the food leaves your stomach, it passes into the duodenum. The lining of the duodenum is ridged.

◀ When food reaches the large intestine it is still mushy. Here, most of the water has been removed and the waste becomes more solid.

the goodness that the body needs to live and grow. There are enough villi in your small intestine to carpet a living room floor! The leftover food mush is then passed into the large intestine. Here water is removed and the waste is stored until it is passed out of the body through the anus.

Facts and Feats

● A meal reaches the large intestine in 5 hours. It takes 24 hours to pass through the gut.

● People who eat only soft foods take a week to digest their food.

● Sometimes methane gas can form in your intestines. This gas is explosive!

● The layer of your gut that absorbs food has an area five times larger than your skin area.

THE FOOD SYSTEM

Waste Matter

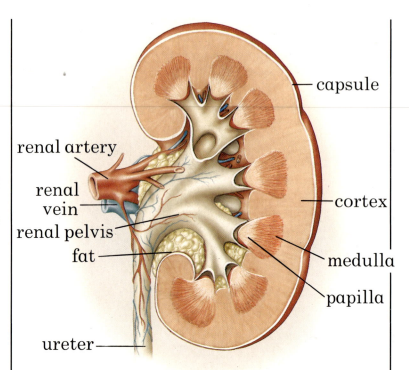

▶ This is a cross-section view of a human kidney. The outer layer, called the cortex, separates blood from chemicals it contains. The urine that results is then sent to the bladder through the ureter.

The solid waste is formed in the large intestine. There are many tiny living microbes in the gut. Some of these keep the gut healthy. By the time the solid waste is ready to be passed out of the body it is partly made of these **microbes**. This food waste is called faeces. It is held in the colon.

The kidneys
Before the faeces are **excreted**, water from them passes into the bloodstream and then to the kidneys. The kidneys filter the blood using tiny structures called

▲ The kidneys are in the small of your back.

36

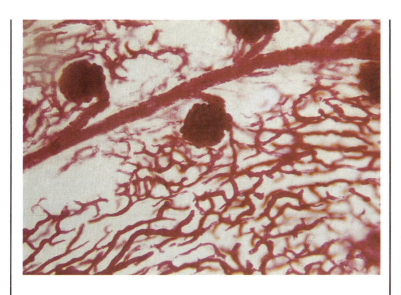

◀ This picture shows a kidney injected with red dye. You can see how many blood vessels there are in the kidney. The dark knots are where the the waste is separated from the blood.

nephrons. All useful substances, such as salt and sugar, are returned to the blood. Unwanted elements are left behind. These then go with any water the body does not need. This liquid called urine is stored in the bladder. Two hundred litres of liquid pass through the kidneys daily. Most of this is re-used by the body.

Did You Know?

● If you were on a starvation diet, you would excrete a minimum of 30 grams of solid waste. If you ate a bulky diet, you would excrete a maximum of 750 grams.

● The food a person eats affects the waste they make. Those who eat a lot of meat have smelly faeces. Vegetable eaters have less smelly faeces, and those who drink only milk do not make a bad smell at all.

◀ When people's kidneys do not work properly, they must use kidney machines to clean their blood. Just think, one small kidney does the job of this huge machine!

The Thymus

CHAPTER FIVE
GLANDS

The thymus gland is located between your upper chest and lower neck. Inside the gland are many white blood cells. These travel through the body in the bloodstream and help to fight off germs. These white blood cells are called **lymphocytes**. The outer part of the thymus, called the cortex, contains many of these lymphocytes.

The mystery gland

No one knows all the jobs the thymus does. As it helps fight disease, it is important for our **immune** system. However, the

▲ This shows the position of the thymus gland. One job of the thymus is to train white blood cells to fight infection.

Did You Know?

● In an experiment, rats were fed pieces of thymus. Their young were large and grew quickly.

● Birds that have no thymus lay soft-shelled eggs.

The Thymus

● Special cells in the thymus help fight germs.

● Some thymus cells die before they can do anything. Others leave the thymus and spread to the rest of the body.

● People with some diseases such as leukaemia or a **goitre** have an extra large thymus. The thymus gland disappears in animals that have become over-exhausted.

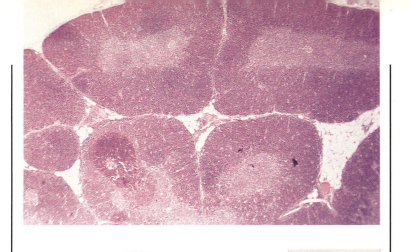

◀ This section of the thymus has been dyed and enlarged. The lymphocytes are the darker cells that form the outer layers of the lobes of the gland.

▲ The thymus gets smaller as people get older. This diagram shows the gland as large in the young and small in the old.

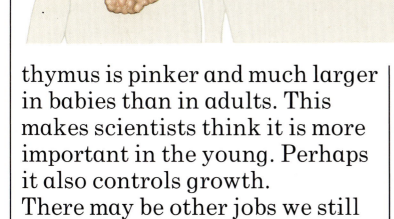

thymus is pinker and much larger in babies than in adults. This makes scientists think it is more important in the young. Perhaps it also controls growth.
There may be other jobs we still do not understand.

▼ In an experiment tadpoles were fed part of a thymus. They grew larger.

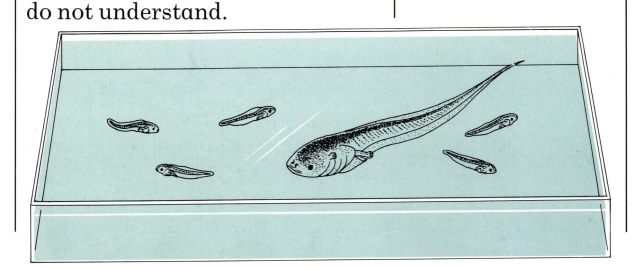

GLANDS

The Third Eye

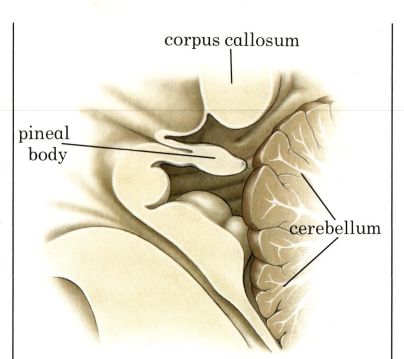

▶ Here is the pineal body, tucked deep inside the brain. It is only the size of a pea.

Deep inside the centre of your brain are two small glands called the pineal body and the pituitary gland. We don't understand everything about the pineal body, but in some animals it acts as an extra eye. In humans, the pineal body seems to react to light. It may be the reason why we feel gloomy on cloudy days and more cheerful when the sun is shining.

The pituitary gland

We know more about the pituitary gland. It makes **hormones** that affect all parts of the body. One important job of these hormones is to help us grow. Children all grow at

Did You Know?

● In some fish the pineal body works like a third eye. In lampreys, it even has a lens. This eye picks up light and the lamprey can change colour to hide itself. Other fish and lizards may have this extra eye as well.

● People who live where winters are dark and long can become depressed. Standing in front of a sun lamp can cheer them up.

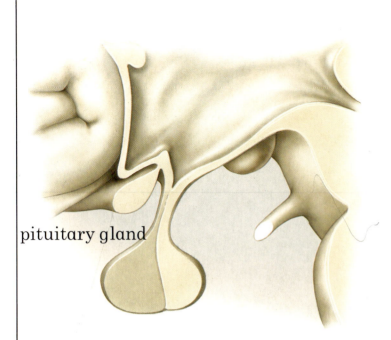

pituitary gland

◀ The pituitary gland is also tucked deep inside the brain. In some ways, it is the master gland of the body because it controls the other glands.

▼ Sandy Allen is much bigger than she should be because her pituitary gland did not work properly.

different speeds. Most children who seem small for their age catch up when their pituitary gland decides it's time for them to grow. In rare cases, the pituitary may not work properly. The person may end up very short or extremely tall.

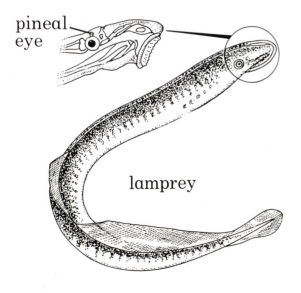

pineal eye

lamprey

◀ The lamprey is a kind of fish. It has a third eye, with a lens and retina.

41

GLANDS

The Thyroid

The thyroid gland grows as two lobes at the base of the neck. Normally, the lobes are the size of two walnut halves. the thyroid gland controls activity. If your thyroid became larger, you would become overactive. If your thyroid slowed down you would become tired and worn out. One experiment showed that tadpoles fed with thyroid **extract** matured into adult frogs much quicker. **Iodine** is necessary to keep the thyroid healthy.

The parathyroid glands

Behind your thyroid are four little glands called the

▲ The base of the neck is where you find the thyroid gland. It wraps around the windpipe.

▶ Here is a front view (left) and back view (right) of the thyroid gland.

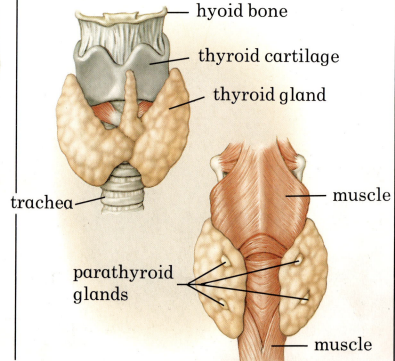

- hyoid bone
- thyroid cartilage
- thyroid gland
- trachea
- muscle
- parathyroid glands
- muscle

42

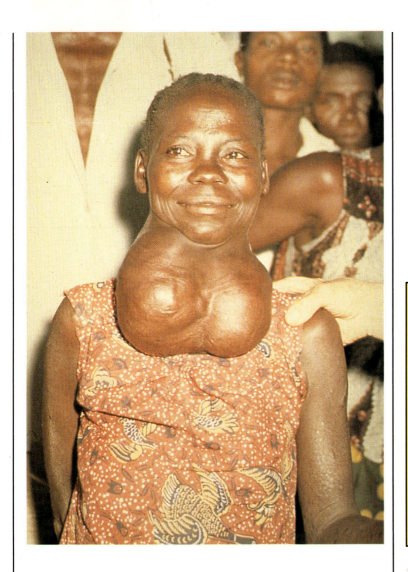

◀ A thyroid gland can grow to a huge size. In countries with few hospitals people can suffer for many years.

Did You Know?

Your thyroid will grow too large if you do not get enough iodine in your diet. In Derby, there is no iodine in the water. For this reason, swollen necks used to be called 'Derbyshire Neck'. Today they use salt that contains iodine.

parathyroid glands. They look a bit like small peas. They help to control the amount of calcium in your body. The proper amount of calcium is necessary to keep bones healthy and strong. People whose parathyroids are overactive become depressed and weak. If your parathyroids were taken out, your muscles would not work properly.

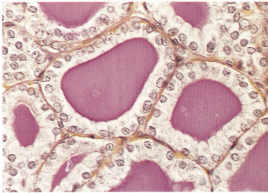

▲ A purple dye has been used to show up the large spaces in the thyroid gland. This is where the hormones are stored.

GLANDS

The Pancreas

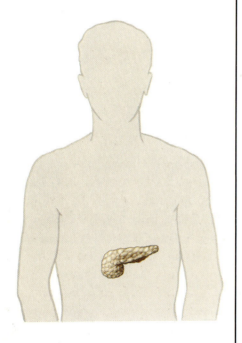

The pancreas makes pancreatic juice. This juice goes into your **duodenum** and helps to digest food. The juice contains **enzymes** that break down proteins into smaller particles. The blood then takes up these usable particles. Other enzymes in the pancreatic juice turn starch into sugar. Fat is also broken down into smaller fatty acids. So you can see how important the pancreas is. The small particles of broken down protein, starch and fat can all be used by the body.

Diabetes
The pancreas tissue is spotted with tiny areas that are different from the rest of the gland. These areas are called the Islets of

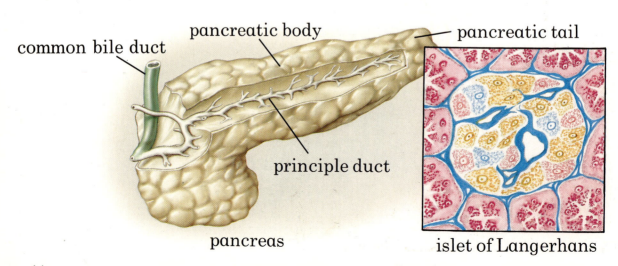

common bile duct — pancreatic body — pancreatic tail
principle duct
pancreas — islet of Langerhans

Langerhans. They aren't really part of the pancreas at all. They are the cells that produce **insulin**. Insulin controls the amount of sugar we have in our blood. When someone has the disease called diabetes, their body makes too much sugar and they become ill. By giving people injections of insulin this illness can be controlled.

◀ The pancreas lies just beneath the stomach. It produces chemicals that help digest food. One of these chemicals is insulin. Insulin is made in a group of cells attached to the pancreas called islets of Langerhans (see diagram opposite). This boy's insulin level is low. He has diabetes. He must give himself a daily injection of insulin to keep himself healthy.

Muscles

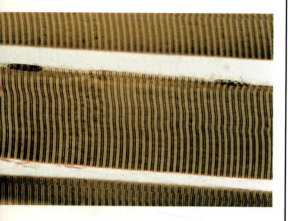

▲ The muscles you can move when you decide to are called voluntary muscles. Under a microscope, these muscles look striped. When you move a muscle, it does not get bigger: the muscle only changes its shape.

CHAPTER SIX
MOVEMENT

Much of the body is made of flesh, or meat. This is muscle. Muscle makes the body move or stay still. You are able to stand or sit still only because your muscles are holding you upright. There are over 600 muscles in the human body. The largest are the gluteus muscles (which you sit on). The smallest are the eye muscles, which you use to follow these words across the page.

How muscles work

Muscles cannot push, they only pull. When you stick out your tongue, muscles are pulling. Your tongue muscles pull in across the tongue, and force it to stick out. Usually muscles do not join directly to the bones they move. Instead, they join onto a **tendon** at the end. It is these tendons that join to bones. Tendons can be 30 or 40 centimetres long, but most are shorter.

There are two different kinds of muscle. Striped, or striated, muscle and smooth muscle.

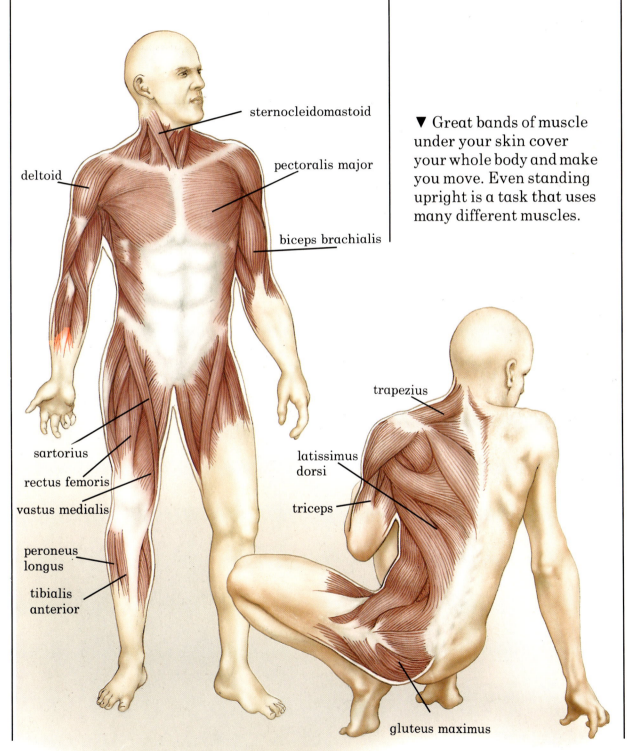

▼ Great bands of muscle under your skin cover your whole body and make you move. Even standing upright is a task that uses many different muscles.

MOVEMENT

Reflexes

Did You Know?

If you put one hand into hot water, and the other into cold water, the reflexes will open or close blood vessels in the skin and allow the hands to get used to the temperature.

▼ Rest one leg over the other, then tap lightly just below the knee-cap. Your leg will jerk up. This is a reflex action that you cannot stop.

Striped muscles control **voluntary** movements. But there is another type of muscle called smooth muscle. These muscles control the automatic movements of your body. These movements are called reflex actions. One example of a reflex action is the knee-jerk reflex.

Protection

Sometimes your body has to react very quickly in order to protect itself. If you touch a very hot object, your hand will draw back very quickly. This happens without you having to think about it. The nerves in your hand pass the message to the spinal cord which sends another message back to the smooth

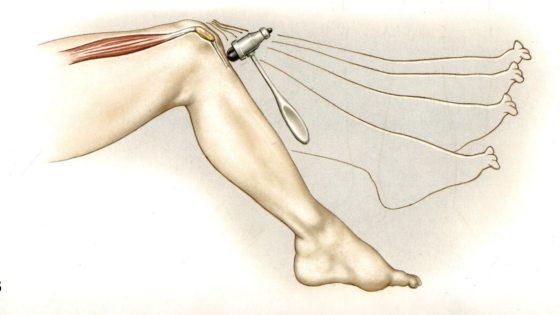

▲ Smooth muscles work automatically. If you are surprised, you will feel hair stand up on the back of your neck. The hair on this coyote is standing on end because it has been frightened. This reflex makes it look bigger to its enemies.

muscles in your arm telling it to pull away. Smooth muscles also have other important jobs. For instance, they keep your food moving automatically in your stomach and intestines. They also control the complicated muscle movements of swallowing.

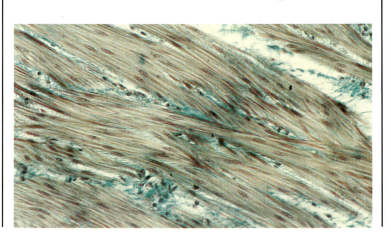

◀ This section from inside the abdomen shows smooth muscle fibres. The body cells are stained with green dyes and the smooth muscle looks grey.

MOVEMENT

The Heart

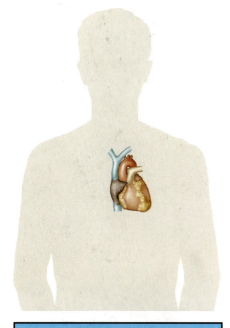

Heart muscle (cardiac muscle) is similar to both smooth and striped muscle. It has some stripes, but you do not have to make your heart beat. Heart beats vary greatly. A bird's heart can beat a 1000 times per minute; an elephant's beats less than 25. An adult human's heart beats about 70 times a minute. The heart is made of four chambers. An adult heart measures about 12 centimetres high, 9 centimetres wide and 6 centimetres deep.

The Heart

- In one minute, about 4 litres of blood make the journey round an adult's body. If the heart pumped for 90 years, it could fill a 200 million litre pool.

- An active athlete can pump 35 litres of blood around the body in a minute.

- Anger or excitement make the heart beat faster than normal.

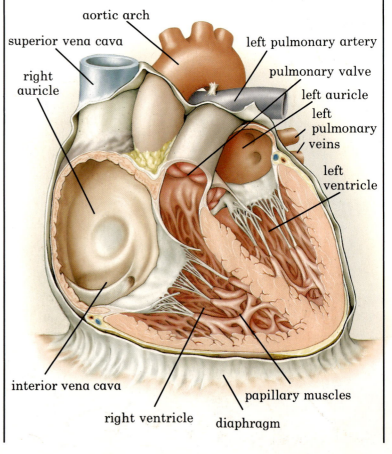

50

How the heart works

Your heart pumps blood around your body. First, blood is pumped from one of the chambers called the right ventricle to the lungs. Here it picks up oxygen. From the lungs, it enters another chamber, the left auricle, and passes down to the left ventricle. It is then pumped into the main blood vessel of the body. From here it passes around the body giving out its oxygen. The blood, now low in oxygen, returns to the right auricle of the heart to start the journey again.

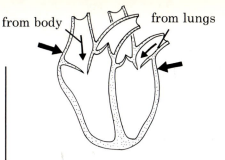
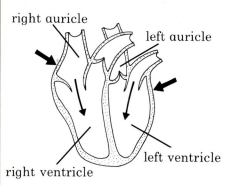
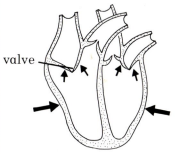
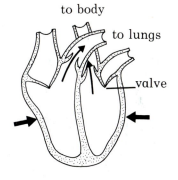

▲ Blood returning from around the body re-enters the auricles. Below these are the muscular ventricles. Muscles in the ventricles jerk together, pushing out the blood with great force.

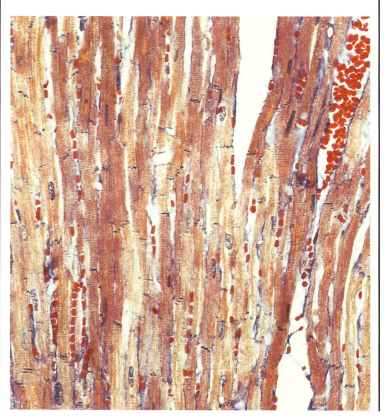

◀ Heart muscle is both striped and smooth.

CHAPTER SEVEN
ON THE OUTSIDE

Hair

▶ These are human hairs greatly enlarged. You can see the scaly surface of the hairs. The shape of these scales varies from person to person

▲ This man has allowed the hair on his face to grow into a beard.

You have about 100,000 hairs on your head. Each one grows from a small pouch on the skin called a follicle. The bottom of the hair, called the root, looks like a rounded bulb. The first hair grows before a baby is born. It is called lanugo, and is very soft. It covers the whole body.

How hair grows

A typical hair follicle makes hair for several years, then stops. The hair withers and falls out within a few days. The follicle then rests for several months before it starts making hair again. Hair grows at the rate of one millimetre every three days. As some people age, they lose their hair or it turns grey. Greying is caused by a hollow space in the centre of hairs that reflects light. Baldness results when hair follicles stop working faster than new ones start up.

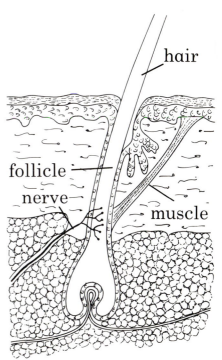

Did You Know?

Hair helps keep you warm. It can also pick up the lightest touch, because nerve endings are wrapped around hair roots (shown above).

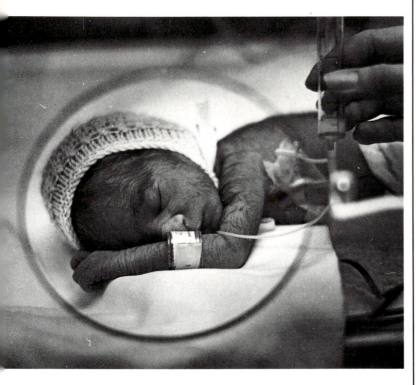

◀ Before babies are born, they are covered with fine, downy hair called lanugo. This tiny baby was born six weeks early. It reminds us of our links with other mammals, most of which stay furry all their lives.

ON THE OUTSIDE

Nails

Nails are made from **keratin**. This is also what turtleshells, feathers, and hair are made from. Nails protect the ends of fingers and toes. Many animals use their nails as weapons. Cats, for example, have very sharp nails called claws. Some people grow

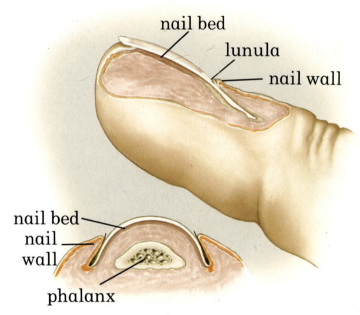

▶ If you could look inside the tip of your finger, you would see the nail bed and the root of the nail. The cross section shows how the opposite nail helps protect the delicate bone at the ends of our fingers.

their nails very long for religious reasons. A man in India stopped cutting his nails in 1952. The average length of his fingernails was over 60 centimetres! His left thumb nail was nearly 75 centimetres long.

How nails grow

Nails are made in the nail-bed. A

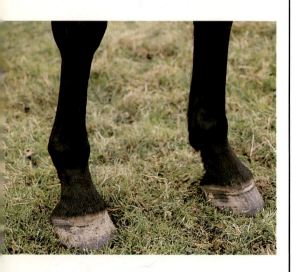

▲ Horse hooves are similar in many ways to human nails. Unlike human nails, horse hooves are very thick and strong.

▲ Human nails can grow to fantastic lengths – up to 30 cms long! They usually break off naturally, though.

special layer inside the skin, called the stratum lucidum, makes the hard nail. At the bottom of the nail is a rounded, pale portion called the lunula. Above the nail at its base is a crescent of the top layer of skin called the cuticle.

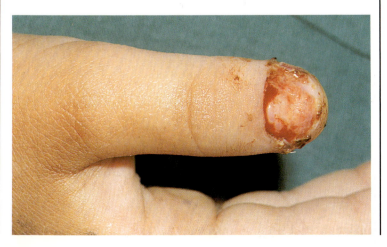

◀ This child lost a nail in an accident. A new nail will grow back in about two months.

ON THE OUTSIDE

Teeth

▶ The first set of teeth are called 'milk teeth'. There are fewer milk teeth than permanent teeth.

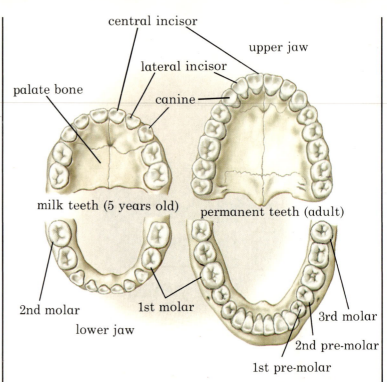

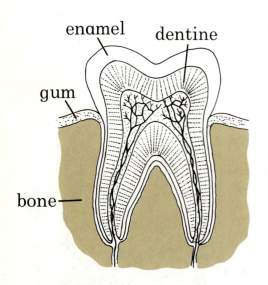

▲ A section through a human tooth shows a hard layer of enamel on the surface. The middle of the tooth has blood vessels and nerves.

Humans grow two sets of teeth. A baby usually has no teeth. The first to grow are milk-teeth, which fall out as an infant becomes a child. The second set are permanent teeth, which may last until old age.

Types of teeth

The teeth at the front of the mouth are called incisors. These have an edge for cutting or biting into food. Next come the sharp canines, which are designed for tearing meat. The wider, grinding teeth are at the back. They are called pre-molars and molars. They are for chewing on food. The

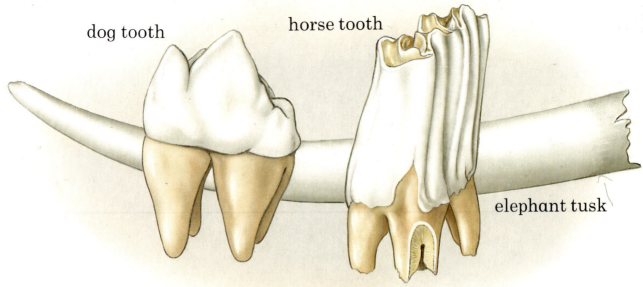

dog tooth
horse tooth
elephant tusk

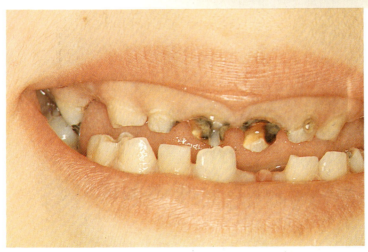

▲ Meat eaters' teeth are sharp, while plant eaters' teeth are flat. An elephant's tusk is actually a very large tooth.

◀ People who do not take care of their teeth can suffer serious tooth decay.

first permanent teeth are the molars. They appear when a child is about six. Adult canines come through at the age of twelve. 'Wisdom teeth', the rear molars, will appear when you are about twenty. Mature teeth are covered with **enamel**, which is the hardest substance in the human body.

What Teeth Arrive When

Name of Tooth	When it comes through (on average)
Lower central incisors	7½ months
Upper central incisors	9½ months
Upper pre-molars	15½ months
Lower pre-molars	16 months
Upper and lower canines	19 months
Second pre-molars	26½ months

CHAPTER EIGHT
BABIES
Giving Birth

7 weeks

3 months

4 months

5 months

6 months

▲ An embryo grows quickly. As the months go by, it becomes a recognizable human. The growing embryo gets food through the placenta.

The egg-cell of a human being is the size of a full stop. It only grows into a baby when it joins with a tiny sperm cell from the father. This is called fertilization.

The developing child
The fertilized egg-cell quickly divides into two. It divides again and again and this grows into a clump of cells called the embryo. By five weeks this is 6 or 7 mm long. Already it has eyes and a heart, which beats rapidly. The developing embryo is connected to the **placenta** by its **umbilical** cord. The placenta is anchored to the inside of the mother's **womb**. The placenta passes food and

Facts and Feats
Babies are usually born head first. A few babies come out feet first. In some rare cases, the baby is lying across the birth canal, trying to come out shoulder first. Sometimes a doctor has to operate to remove the baby. A cut is made and the baby is lifted out. This operation is called a 'Caesarian'.

oxygen from the mother's blood to the baby's blood. It also gets rid of the baby's wastes by passing them through the mother's bloodstream.

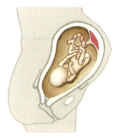  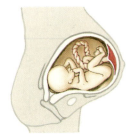 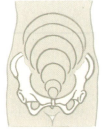

7 months   8 months   9 months (ready for birth)   front view expanding womb

Birth

The mother's body can tell when the baby is fully formed. Soon the mother will go into labour. This is a long period when muscles in the womb **contract** with increasing force. Then the baby is pushed through the vagina, between the mother's legs. This miracle of birth starts our story afresh.

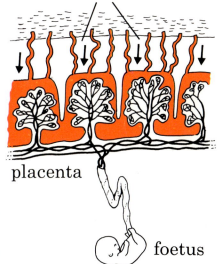

▲ Blood from the mother is filtered through the placenta.

◀ At the end of nine months, the growing mass of cells enters the world as a wonderful new baby.

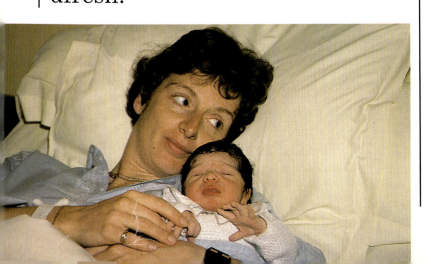

Glossary

Carbohydrates: sugar and starch are carbohydrates. They are a useful supply of energy to the body.
Carbon dioxide: this is an invisible and colourless gas in our air. It has no taste or smell.
Cartilage: a strong but bendy tissue that gives support to the body.
Cell: the smallest part of a living thing that is capable of life. Cells are the basic building blocks from which all living things are made.
Cones: cells at the back of the eye that pick up colours from bright light.
Digestion: the process by which food is broken down in the stomach and gut and is made useful to the body.
Duodenum: the part of the gut that comes directly from the stomach.
Enzyme: a substance produced in the body. Enzymes change one substance into another but remain unchanged themselves.
Excrete: to pass a waste product out of the body. When you go to the lavatory, you excrete waste products.
Extract: this is a word to describe a part that has been taken from a larger whole.
Gland: a part of the body that makes chemical substances that are useful to the body; the thyroid gland and sweat glands are examples.
Goitre: this is a word used to describe a swelling in front of the throat. It is caused by an enlarged thyroid gland.
Hormones: chemical messengers that are released by certain glands and carried by the bloodstream to produce effects in other parts of the body.
Hydrochloric acid: a burning liquid that helps to break down food into useful substances in the stomach.
Immune system: all bodies have natural defences against disease and germs. These defences are known as the immune system.
Insulin: a chemical substance produced inside the pancreas. It controls sugar levels in the body.
Iodine: a chemical that occurs naturally in food. It is necessary to keep the thyroid gland healthy.
Lobes: roundish, sticking out parts of something, such as the ear lobes. The brain is divided into lobes.
Lymphocytes: a type of white blood cell found in all parts of the body except the nervous system. They are an important part of the body's defences against disease.
Membrane: a thin, flexible sheet-like part of the body. It either connects different organs or lines an organ.
Microbes: a tiny living thing, either plant or animal.
Mucin: a slimy substance which lines the mouth, nose, lungs and gut of the body.
Organ: part of the body that does particular jobs. For instance, the heart pumps blood around the body.
Organ of Corti: a spiral organ inside the cochlea. It was named after its discoverer. It vibrates with sounds which nerve fibres pick up and send to the brain.
Oxygen: an invisible gas that has no taste or smell. Animals could not breathe without it.
Placenta: a spongy, flattened circular organ attached to the lining of the mother's womb. The baby receives all the food and oxygen it needs through the placenta.

Protein: a complex substance that is essential to all living things. It is important to many different parts of the body.

Rods: cells at the back of the eye that pick up black and white in dim light.

Saliva: the colourless liquid produced in the mouth. It starts the digestive process, by breaking down certain parts of our food.

Sever: this word means to cut or separate something.

Spinal cord: this is the length of nerve fibres that run up to the brain along the vertebrae of the spine. It is a vital part of the body since it joins the brain and the rest of the body.

Stimulus: something that makes a living thing or organ act or respond in a certain way.

Tendon: a non-stretching band that links muscle to bone.

Tissue: one of the various parts of the body. Tissues are made up of similar types of cell working together to do particular jobs.

Umbilical: of or coming from the navel (belly button). The umbilical cord is the link between the mother's placenta and the unborn child.

Valve: a fold or flap in an organ or passage of the body that controls the flow of some liquid, such as blood. It closes like a trapdoor to prevent fluids returning in the opposite directiion.

Vibrate: to shake slightly or tremble.

Virus: a tiny living thing that causes disease. They are possibly the smallest living thing.

Vitamins: complex substances that are essential for the body to work properly. Lack of vitamins in the diet will lead to disease.

Voluntary: this word describes an act that is done deliberately. The person has thought about it and decided to do it. For example you can decide to kick a football (or not).

Womb: the part of a woman's body in which the unborn baby is held and protected during pregnancy.

Index

A number in **bold** shows the entry is illustrated on that page. The same page often has writing about the entry too.

Aa
abdomen **32**, 49
alveoli **19**
ankles **6**
anus 35
aorta **14**
appendix **35**
arms **6**, 7, 48-49
arteries **14**, **50**
axons 13

Bb
babies **53**, 58-59
balancing **23**
bats 22
bile duct **14**, **15**, **44**
bladder 36, 37
blindspot **20**, 21
blood, the **5**, 26, **37**, 59
   cells **14-15**
      red 7, **15**, 18
      white **15**, 38, **39**
   system **9**, **16**, **17**
   villi **34**
body, the 4-5
bones **5**, **6**, **7**, **29**
brain, the 9, **10**, **11**, 25, 40
   and seeing 21
breathing 18-**19**, 30-**31**

Cc
calcium 6, 43
canines (teeth) **56**, 57
carbohydrates 34
carbon dioxide 19
cardiac muscle 50, **51**
carotene 15
carpus (wrist bone) **6**, 7

cells 38
   blood 7, 14-**15**, 18, 38, **39**
   brain **10**, 11
   egg 5, 28, 58
   nerve **12**, 13
   skin 27
cerebellum **10**, 11
cerebral cortex **10**, 11
coccyx (tail bone) **6**
cochlea 22, **23**
colon **35**, 36
cones 21
Corti, organ of 22-23
coyote, frightened **49**
cuticle 54

Dd
dentine **56**
dermis (skin layer) **27**
diabetes 44-**45**
dialysis machine **37**
digestion 28, 34-35
dogs 22, **57**
duodenum **35**
dust mites 26

Ee
ears, the 8, **22-23**
egg cells 5, 28, 58
elbows **6**
elephants 50
   brain **11**
   tusk **57**
embryo **58-59**
enamel **56**, 57
epidermis (skin layer) **27**
epiglottis **30**, **31**
eustachian tubes 29
eyes, the 8, **20**, **21**, 46

Ff
faeces 36
feet **6**
femur (leg bone) **6**, 7
fertilization 58

fibula (leg bone) **6**
fingerprints 26
fingers **6**, **7**, **54**, **55**
follicles, hair 27, 52, **53**
frenulum 28
frontal lobes (brain) **10**, 11

Gg
gall bladder **14**
glands 38-45
    liver **14**, **15**
    oil 27
    pancreas **44**-**45**
    the pineal body **10**, **40**, **41**
    saliva 28
    sublingual **29**
    sweat **26-27**
    the thymus **38**, **39**
    the thyroid **42**, **43**
gluteus muscles 46, **47**
growing 6, 11, **38-41**, **58-59**
gum **56**
gut, the **34**, 35

Hh
haemoglobin 18
hair 5, **27**, **52**, **53**
hands **6**, **7**, 48
heart, the 4, **14**, **50**, **51**
hips **6**, **7**, 7
Homo sapiens (wise man) **5**
horses **54**, **57**
humerus (arm bone) **6**
hydrochloric acid 32, **33**

Ii
immune system 38
incisors (teeth) **56**
infections, fighting 15, 17
insulin **44-45**
intestines, the **33**, **34**, **35**
islets of Langerhans **44-45**

Jj
jaws **6**, **8**, **9**, **29**

Kk
keratin 54
kidneys, the **36**, **37**
knee-jerk reflex **48**

Ll
lampreys 40, **41**
Langerhans, islets of **44-45**
lanugo (babies' hair) **53**
larynx 30, **31**
legs **6**, **7**
lens **20**, **41**
liver, the **14**, **15**, 34
lungs, the **18**, **19**, 51
lymphocytes **15**, **38**, **39**

Mm
metacarpus (finger bone) **6**, **7**
metatarsus (foot bone) **6**
'milk teeth' **56**
molars (teeth) **56**, **57**
mouth, the **25**, **28**, **29**
movement 4, 11, 26, **46-47**
mucin 33
muscles 7, **29**, **42**, **46**, **47**, 59
    cardiac 50, **51**
    hair **53**
    intestine 33
    stomach 33

Nn
nails **54**, **55**
nerves **5**, **12**, **13**, **48**, **53**, 56
    skin **27**
nose, the **24**

Oo
œsophagus **30**, **35**
optic nerve **20**
ossicles (ear bones) 22
oxygen 18, **19**, 51, 59

Pp
palate **24**, **30**
pancreas, the **44**, 45

parathyroid glands **42**-43
patella (knee joint) **6**
pelvis (hip bone) **6**, 7
phalanges (toes) **6**
pharynx (upper throat) 30
pineal body (third eye) **10**, **40**, **41**
pituitary gland 40, **41**
placenta 58, **59**
platelets **17**
pre-molars (teeth) **56**

Rr
radius (arm bone) **6**
reflexes **13**, 30, **48**-49
retina 41
ribs **6**, 14
rods 21

Ss
saliva 28
shoulder blades **6**
skeleton, human **6**
skin 5, **26**-**27**
skull, the **6**, 7, 8, **9**
smell **24**-**25**
sperm cell 58
spinal cord 7, **12**, 13, 48
spine, the **6**, 7
stomach, the **32**, **33**
stratum lucidum (nail-bed) **54**-55
swallowing 30, **31**, 49
sweat glands 26-**27**

Tt
tadpoles **39**, 42
tarsus (ankle bone) **6**
taste 24, **25**
teeth **56**, **57**
temperature control 26-27
tendons 46
thigh bone **7**
throat, the **30**, **31**
thymus, the **38**, **39**
thyroid, the **42**, **43**
tibia (leg bone) **6**

toes **6**, 7, 54
tongue, the **25**, **28**, **29**
tonsils 29
tooth decay **57**
touch 26-27
trachea (windpipe) **18**, **42**

Uu
ulna (arm bone) **6**
umbilical cord **58**, **59**
urine 36

Vv
veins **14**
vertebrae (back bones) **6**, 7
villi (blood vessels) **34**
vitamins 15, 34
vitreous humour **20**
vocal cords **31**
voluntary muscles **46**, **47**, 48

Ww
waste matter 19, 35, **36**-**37**, 59
windpipe **18**, **42**
womb, the **58**, **59**
wrist, the **6**, **7**